PEACE
ON EARTH?

Relax Christian, God still has your back.

DAVID MAY

DEDICATION

This is dedicated to my dad, Cecil May, who was the most peaceful man I have known, and to his son, my brother, by the same name who has followed in the footsteps of both our spiritual and our earthly fathers.

TABLE OF CONTENTS

PART 1

PEACE VS. FEAR, ANGER, AND THE AMERICAN DREAM

"This world is not my home; I'm just a passing through."[1]

Traditional

CHAPTER 1

INTRODUCTION TO PART 1

Christians are called to be a peaceful people in an unpeaceful world. Yet at times we seem to be the least peaceful people around. What is at work here, and what should we be doing to correct the situation?

Are peaceful Christians an oxymoron? The beginning of this book is a discussion of the nature of the peace God promised us and of the reasons we seem to have difficulty claiming that peace. We will think together about some of the opponents to peace in our lives like anger and fear and our American desire to run our own lives.

It is intentionally a short book with the hope that its brevity will encourage you and others to read it. Its importance lies in part in its intention to redirect the church's attention away from the hair pulling about "righteous legislation" and instead toward righteous teaching. Much more could be written on many of the topics addressed here, but these thoughts are presented as an illustration of some basic principles in the direction of the work of the church.

I have written two books challenging church members to get up out of the pews and charge out into the streets to carry God's message of love and to help whomever we see that can use some help. So why am I now counseling Christians to relax? Am I saying we should leave the pews and go home to the couch? No, not really.

But, as we go about the essential and urgent business of the church, we should do it in a way that instills confidence. We must approach the world calmly and with assurance. If we run around like Chicken Little proclaiming that the sky is falling, or that the foundation is crumbling under our nation, many will not believe us about that, or about anything else we have to say. We need to focus our message on Jesus and on him alone as Paul indicated in the first Corinthian letter.[2]

We need to be peaceful and bold at the same time. We are not called to be reluctant messengers. God does not want us to be ashamed of the Gospel.[3] Being bold, yet peaceful in our service to God seems a tricky proposition, one that requires a bit of balancing. We will talk about maintaining that balance without tipping one way or the other.

Toward the end of the book I write about what some would call political matters. I would refer to that part of the book though as being "anti-political." I operate from the position that God called on us to change the world by our preaching. teaching, and example;[4] not by legislating people into righteousness. Much more could be said about each of the topics in that section,

---

2   1 Corinthians 2:2
3   Romans 1:16
4   1 Corinthians 1:20-22

but these quick points are offered as thought provokers and discussion starters, not as the final word. Whether you agree with that section or not, it makes an interesting read. Hopefully it will cause you to think somewhat differently about what we read and hear so often from politicians and political activists these days.

This is a book about being peaceful, confident messengers of God's communication to the people around us. I hope it will be an encouragement to you that we don't have to be nervous and fearful about our assignment here. God still has our backs

CHAPTER 2

PEACE ON EARTH

*"Whatever my lot, thou hast taught me to say,
it is well with my soul."*[5]

---

5   Words: Horatio Spafford, 1873. Music: Philip Bliss, 1876.

AN ANNOUNCEMENT OF PEACE THAT DIDN'T SEEM TO WORK OUT THAT WAY

When the angels came to announce the birth of Jesus, they called it an announcement of "peace on earth."[6] Yet what ensued was an attempt on the baby's life, hundreds of children being slaughtered, and Jesus' family having to go into the witness protection program in a country that was famous for having enslaved his ancestors.

During his ministry, Jesus was dogged by religious leaders and finally falsely accused (though not very convincingly) and put to death. Peace on earth? What were the angels talking about? Jesus left us with a bit of a riddle on the matter of peace didn't he?

THE PUZZLE

First he called on us to be a peace-loving, peace-making people. And when he appointed us as peace-makers there was no indication that what he had in mind was the 1873 Colt .45 revolver called the Peacemaker. In a sense, that old firearm could be called a "peacemaker" in the hands of a lawman, but Jesus wanted us to make peace without us becoming the instrument of the civil

---

6   Luke 2:14

law. He put us at a bit of a disadvantage in relation to the marshals of the old west.

He started his sermon on the mount with a blessing for those who will go out of their way to make peace. "… for they shall be called sons of God."[7] Then only five chapters later, he said he did not come to bring peace[8]. In that more direct reference, Jesus spoke of us taking up a cross and losing our lives for his sake – an image of martyrs. Not a very peaceful reference.

PEOPLE AT PEACE IN A TROUBLED WORLD

We are called to be a people of peace, but Jesus didn't come to bring peace. How does that work? I am reminded of a story I heard long ago. Imagine a very peaceful scene. You are on the beach, the sun is shining, there is a gentle breeze, and a small bird is singing away from the swaying branches of a nearby tree. Peaceful, no?

Now imagine the same beach with a hurricane offshore. The waves are crashing onto the beach, the sky is dark, and the trees are creaking and jerking violently. And

---

7   Matthew 5:9
8   Matthew 10:34-39

from somewhere the little bird is still there, singing
his heart out. The bird has peace inside; he does not
derive it from whatever is going on around him. I
don't know whether birds really sing during a storm,
but it's an illustrative story. Like the bird is how we are
called on to live. Jesus doesn't promise us a peaceful
world[9], but he calls on us to be at peace in that world.
Paul described how to pull it off in his letter to the
Philippians when he said, "for I have learned to be content in whatever circumstances I am. I know how to
get along with humble means, and I also know how
to live in prosperity; in any and every circumstance I
have learned the secret of being filled and going hungry, both of having abundance and suffering need."[10]

I was recently in a study with several preachers, most
of us older guys, having been at it for awhile. The
discussion was about Jesus' notion of peace and about
how we are to approach the world with gentleness [11]
Please understand that preachers are frequently belea-
guered by opposition from within their congregations.
They are often unsure how best to respond, uncertain
when to stand their ground and when to compromise
to "keep the peace."

---

9   John 14:27
10   Philippians 4:11-12
11   For example Galatians 5:22-23; Philippians 4:5-6

Sometimes when they are with other preachers is the only time they can truly open up and describe what they see happening to them. In that context, our little preachers' discussion became a very emotional time. There were tears as some of us examined our personal responses to Jesus' calling to be peacemakers in an un-peaceful world. It is a hard charge the Lord has given us.

WHAT IS PEACE?

Can you define something just by saying what it is not? That is how we often try to define peace. Is it the absence of conflict? Is it the absence of trouble or fear? Those are certainly a part of it, but it has to be more than that, because Jesus made it clear that he did not come to bring that kind of peace. He promises us trouble in this world[12] and then says we should have courage because he has overcome the world. A big part of the definition of peace has to be our courage. He asks us to be a courageous people in the face of opposition and hard times.

A courageous people will see trouble in a different light. We will see difficulty as just a part of the road we need to travel to get to where we are going. If we

---

12   John 16:32-33

are headed to heaven we will encounter opposition. If we are going on a mission for God's kingdom, we will run into natural obstacles as well as those placed there by people who don't want to see us succeed.

CHECHERONE

A few years ago I was in Haiti and was asked to speak somewhere that I had never been. Checherone is at the top of a steep mountain. About half way up there is a little village, but as you near the top of the mountain there is little evidence that anyone lives there. Finally the trail comes to an end and as you look up to the right, there is a large green building. It is where the church meets, a group of about 400. Because of the difficulty in getting there, they have few visitors.

A few years earlier the preacher who had founded the church had told them that if they were not a part of the big city church where he lived, they were not really the church. He was trying to start a denomination and wanted them to be a part of it – to contribute to his group. The young preacher who was working with them had parents and a grandfather who lived there and he was anxious for them to hear from me that their founder was wrong. He had told them, but he was a young preacher trying to refute what the older, more "successful" man had told them. So I agreed to go. We were dropped off in the little village at the bottom of the mountain. The big truck that left us there could not have negotiated the little donkey trail very well and was needed elsewhere that weekend. The preacher knew a man with a vehicle (a "machine" in Creole) who would take us up.

We sat around and waited at least an hour and a half while the friend tried to get the vehicle started. When he finally did, we all piled in: two preachers, one preacher's wife and two daughters, the driver, and me - all in a small car with stuff to spend two nights and other stuff they were taking to the grandparents who lived there. The car ran okay with sputters and jerks as long as we were on level ground. But as soon as we got to the mountain it quit. The rest of the day was spent with the driver's head under the hood (and sometimes others of us). The machine would go a couple of hundred yards then quit again. The road was steep, narrow and very rough. Most would not call it a road at all. It was more of a mountain path.

Several times all the guys were in back pushing and once they tied the middle of a rope to the front bumper and the guys made a V of the rope with men on both sides trying to pull the machine up the mountain. When we got close to the destination after dark, someone picked me up on a motor cycle which we got on and off of from time to time depending on the grade. The other guys walked up the rest of the way.

We finally got to the little church late in the evening, long after I was supposed to speak. The next morning I told the church that we would have been there much sooner had we started out to walk and hadn't had to push and pull the machine up the mountain. Eventually the machine got to the meeting place. It proved to be better for a downhill ride than it was at going up the grade.

The issue with the teaching the church was receiving from their former preacher continues. My contribution as an "expert from the states" was minor, but may have served to relieve some of them of some of their anxiety. The young preacher will continue to bring in others to support the scriptural view of the situation, and so far they have not given in and joined the older fellow's new denomination.

Satan will indeed put obstacles in your way when you set out to do what's right. The New Testament from Luke to Revelation is full of encouragement for us to be people who persevere.[13] Likewise Jesus was constantly

---

13   2 Thessalonians 1:4; 2 Peter 1;6

calling on his followers to have courage.[14] He doesn't want us giving up just because we have discovered that the task is bigger than we are. "God is bigger than the boogie man."

Courage will lead us to expect *whatever* happens. If we are expecting an undefined difficulty, when it comes we will not be thrown by it. We will take it in stride, step around it or climb over it and stay the course. This world is not our home and we need not be too concerned about it.

PEACE IN THREE DIMENSIONS

1. We live in a violent and oppositional world, a place where to be a Christian is to invite ridicule and in some places even attacks on our lives. And even where the animosity is not so blatant, our values are opposed by the very culture in which we live, work, and raise our children.

2. Yet we are asked to be at peace in that world.[15] Our peace is one that is beyond understanding in the context in which we live.[16] It comes from our understanding

---

14   Matthew 9:2&22; John 16:33
15   Romans 12:18
16   Philippians 4:7

that this world is not our home.[17] Like Abraham and all the other heroes of Hebrews 11, we are looking for a better home. Indeed we know we already are living out our eternal life. Our savior has overcome the world.[18] He got up and walked out of the grave on a Sunday morning proving once, for all time, that we have nothing in this world to be afraid of.

3. But beyond being at peace in an un-peaceful world, we are called on to be peacemakers. We are to bring peace where there is no peace. I must assume that the nature of the peace we are to impart on the world around us is not so much a temporal peace (an absence of crime, violence, name calling and accusing) as it is a peace like the one we carry with us. It is a peace that comes from our view of the world as a temporary residence – a place where we have a job to do, and a place from which we will depart to go home when our mission is done.

---

17   Hebrews 11:8-10, 13-16, 32-40
18   John 16:33

CHAPTER 3

UNFORTUNATELY CHRISTIANS ARE NOT KNOWN AS PEACEFUL PEOPLE

"Peace, perfect peace, in this dark world of sin: The blood of Jesus whispers peace within."[19]

19 Words: Edward H Bickersteth, 1875; Music: George T Caldbeck, 1877

WHOSE FAULT?

We have made the case that Christians should be a peaceful people, but those around us might not be so quick to label us as peace loving. That may not be our fault at all. It may lie at the feet of a handful of highly visible "Christian Leaders." But even if that is true, to the extent that we follow these leaders, echo their war cries, forward their accusatory emails, and link to their trouble-making web pages, we are contributing to the view that Christian people are indeed looking to make trouble rather than to bring peace.

What do outsiders think of us? Those who know us well may think we are soft-headed nice people with good hearts. Maybe they have heard of our mission trips and our generosity. Perhaps they like us okay, but think we are a little strange and they have determined to just stay away from religious conversation with us.

ARE WE "THE RELIGIOUS RIGHT"?

Others though draw their conclusions from what they have seen in the news and read on-line. They see us first as wrong-headed about the social issues of the day and then as vicious fighters for what we see as right. The issues from their view are largely about individuals' rights and personal freedoms - the founding principles of our nation. And they believe our attacks on those rights are an affront to the fundamental foundations of our society. They see us as unfriendly because we want to use the government to limit citizens' civil liberties and control things like who you can marry, what you can do with your body and whether you can even live in our country.

Our positions on abortion, gay rights, immigration, even war and homeland security have become confused in their minds with the positions of the Republican Party or the Tea Party. The vocal ranting of party leaders, bloggers and pundits, often using Christian arguments, are all lumped in their minds as the mistaken and evil intentioned tirades of what they call the "religious right." Bear with me now. If you throw the book away at this point, you may just be proving their point.

To the extent that we have identified with the ravings of people who are not willing to have a discussion with the other side, people who talk like they have all the answers and see their mission as shouting down the "evil opposition," we do severe damage to the picture of us as peacemakers that Jesus was trying to paint. We need to distinguish ourselves from these folks.

Jesus did not commission his disciples to "Go into all the world and enforce a moral code on every creature, regardless of whether they are believers or not."[20] Remember the Colt Peacemaker revolver.

He did say that if we love him we will keep his commandments.[21] We get people to do that by telling them the good news. We are to teach them about Jesus' love for them and we are to coach them into a love for Jesus. *Then* they will keep his commandments.[22]

Do you see the difference? On the one hand we are making laws to get people to act in moral ways, whether they are inclined that way or not. Keeping a moral code because the government will punish us if we don't is not the New Testament goal.

On the other hand if we are telling people about Jesus and are holding up his standards as the proper goal for Godly people, we will be able to bring about willing adherence to the moral codes of the Bible.

BEING A PEACEFUL PEOPLE

How do we make ourselves known as a peaceful people in the midst of all this disagreement about how much

---

20   Mark 16:15
21   John 14:15
22   1 John 2:3-6

authority the government should have to regulate the lives of its citizens? I really don't like this answer, but it seems to be the truth. We do it one conversation at a time. Just as Jesus sent us out to teach the good news to people, we have to show the same people that we are a loving people and are a people of peace. That is a demonstration that is most effectively given one on one.

And to the extent that we have a larger audience, say our church group, our family, or a blog readership, we can make our peaceful nature known there. This, though, is a tricky endeavor. Not carefully done, it can come across as "I am a peace loving person and you are not and if you don't straighten up I will punch you in the nose." Entering the argument to tell both quarrelers that they are wrong and we are right and they need to listen to us will only make the situation worse.

Peace wins by being peaceful. The peace that we have is an attractive trait. Many people will want to know more about it. Some will want to know how to acquire it. That is the course we need to take. And as more of us take that path, our influence will grow.

There are so many angry people around today, it is hard to imagine that a handful of peaceful people can make a difference, but what else can work? We need to be assertive peace makers, in your face peacemakers, interveners who will step in to cut off a loud disagreement and encourage people to at least listen to each other. Micro-interventions repeated again and again eventually turn into macro-interventions.

Oh, and take the time to encourage anyone you see who is being an active peace maker.

CHAPTER 4

THE PROPER PLACE FOR ANGER

"For the churning of milk produces butter,
And pressing the nose brings forth blood;
So the churning of anger produces strife."[23]

---

23   Proverbs 30:33

THE PROPER PLACE FOR ANGER

WHAT MAKES YOU ANGRY?

Is your anger most related to how the boss treats you? The insensitivity of your coworkers? The lack of understanding your spouse has for you? Your kids' lack of respect or their laziness? Traffic? I am guessing it is mostly about how other people treat you.

Our anger is closely related to our fear. Often we are angry about whatever we are afraid of. Anger covers the fear. We come on strong and push back on the situation or person who scares us and it protects us from confronting our fear. In that way, anger is destructive to the person who exhibits it, because it covers the underlying emotion and prevents us from having to deal with it. Without the anger, we could meet our fears head on, but anger prevents us from doing so.

Did you ever flare up at someone you love, quickly and without warning, and then be amazed at yourself? "Where did that come from?" you wonder. And when you examine the situation, the anger rose from something the other person did or said that triggered old fears – maybe honest fears for how the person will turn out, or that they will stop loving you, or that they will not find their way into heaven or that their attitude toward you will embarrass you in the eyes of others. And those fears in turn triggered the anger.

A LITTLE OR A LOT MAKES NO DIFFERENCE

Some of us go through life showing very little anger. For whatever reason, temperament maybe, it just takes a lot to make us mad. And when the door to our anger is opened, it is often sudden, loud, maybe out of control. But it is short lived. Then we are under control again. Our burst of anger itself scares us. It is inconsistent with our view of ourselves and we hurry to bury it again.

Others of us wear our anger on our sleeves. Anything, it seems can touch it off and no one is safe from its consequences. But whichever category describes our anger, or whether we are somewhere in between, it is still not a part of who God calls us to be.

Now that is a powerful statement: "God does not call us to be angry." But I believe it to be true. If we can begin to understand how God calls us to deal with fear and anger, we will begin to take our places as effective citizens in his kingdom. We need to eliminate these barriers to our service to him.

"BE ANGRY AND SIN NOT."

Okay so Ephesians 4:26 says to be angry. How can we argue with that? Well, the context is a call to righteousness. In the larger passage we are called to quit lying and stealing. Paul does give us enough leeway to get legitimately angry if we must, but then he says in the same verse not to go to bed angry. Then in verses 31 and 32 he says we should put away from us all bitterness, wrath, and *anger*, and we should instead be kind, tenderhearted, and forgiving. So this passage is clearly not a call to anger.

WAS JESUS' CLEARING OF THE MONEYCHANGERS FROM THE TEMPLE AN ACT OF ANGER?

Another Biblical passage sometimes used to justify anger is Jesus' clearing of the temple.[24] But if you read the passages carefully, clearing the temple follows immediately after his triumphal entry into Jerusalem. The people were crying out "Hosanna! Hosanna!" And when he got into town he went directly to the temple. Nowhere in the three accounts does it say he saw the money changers and got angry.

In the Mark account it says he went in one day and looked around and saw everything that was there. He then left the temple, went to Bethany to spend the night, and came back and cleaned it out the next day.

---

24   Matthew 21:12-16; Mark 11:15-18; Luke 19:45-47; John 2:13-17

The John account says he made a whip of cords before
he cleaned it out. Some commentators believe there
were two events when Jesus drove the money changers
out of the temple. That discussion is not relevant to
our purposes here. Whether it was once or twice, it
seems very deliberate – going in and seeing it one day
and coming back to clean it out the next – taking time
to make a whip. Neither of these events reads like he
saw something that made him lose his temper. They
seem very deliberate.

Yes cleaning the money changers out of the temple
was an authoritative act on behalf of his father, who
owned the place, but it does not really read like an act
of anger.

Hebrews 3:17 says God was angry with his people
for 40 years, but we are called on to turn loose of our
anger by nightfall. That is okay with me. God has
a right to be angry with whomever he chooses. He
was angry at sin.[25] If we are angry at a brother (the
implication is that we harbor ongoing anger) we are
in danger of the judgment.[26] I get the impression
that anger is primarily God's job and we are to be
peacemakers.

---

25   Hebrews 3:17
26   Matthew 5:22

Jesus angry at the Pharisees

But Jesus is our example and we do know that he was
angry at least once – at the Pharisees.[27] He was in the
synagogue on the Sabbath and a man was there with
a withered hand. Jesus, as he frequently did when he
met someone who had some infirmity, wanted to heal
the man. But the Pharisees were watching to see if
he would heal on the Sabbath. If he did, they would
accuse him of violating one of their rules. Yes the
Sabbath was God's rule, but they had interpreted it
very narrowly, and then forced that interpretation on
the people. They interpreted this "religious rule" in
such a way as to prevent people (Jesus in this case) from
doing what was really God's overall, summary rule –
helping someone who needed help.

Jesus did not secretly heal the man's hand; he called
him to the front of the room. Once Jesus and the man
were standing together, in front of all the people, Jesus
asked the crowd whether it was "lawful" under their
law to do good or evil on the Sabbath. No one gave
an answer. At that point John records that Jesus was
both angry at them and grieved because of their hard
hearts. Jesus loved even these hypocritical religious
leaders who set out to trap him and eventually to kill

---

27   Mark 3:1-6

him. He was grieved because they would not understand what he was teaching. And he was angry. What did he do with his anger? He did what he would have done anyway. He healed the man – so everyone could see. He asked whether it was lawful to do good or evil, then he did good. That looks like an example of how we can "be angry and sin not."[28] We should continue to love the person we are angry with (he was grieved) and we should turn our anger into energy to do the right thing.

ANGER GIVES US ENERGY

Anger triggers the "fight or flight" response in us. It releases chemicals to prepare our bodies for action. Our job at that point is to direct that readiness toward something good – toward helping someone as Jesus did. If we are angry because someone cut us off in traffic, we can redirect that energy not only toward letting him or her into our lane, but also letting in the next two or three people.

God acknowledged that the emotional makeup he created for us includes the anger response just as it does the sexual response and fear. But he asks us to be in

---

28   Ephesians 4:26

control of it and not vice versa. We are to be known as people of peace.

If we follow Jesus' example, our anger will be directed at injustice, and as Isaiah wrote, we can aim that energy at correcting unfairness:

"Is this not the fast which I choose,
To loosen the bonds of wickedness,
To undo the bands of the yoke,
And to let the oppressed go free
And break every yoke?"
"Is it not to divide your bread with the hungry
And bring the homeless poor into the house;
When you see the naked, to cover him;
And not to hide yourself from your own flesh?"[29]

---

29   Isaiah 58:6-7

CHAPTER 5

WHAT IS THE PROPER PLACE FOR FEAR IN OUR LIVES?

"God is bigger than the boogie man,
He's bigger than Godzilla or the monsters on TV,
Oh, God is bigger than the boogie man,
And he's watching out for you and me- ee-ee, hey!"

- Junior Asparagus[30]

---

30   http://en.wikipedia.org/wiki/Junior_Asparagus#Junior_Asparagus

Enough said. God is indeed bigger than anything in this world that we might choose to be afraid of. Jesus has overcome the world. He said so.[31] And he tied that directly to his desire that we be at peace *in the world*. He was not talking about some esoteric peace in the sky bye and bye. In the same verse where he spoke of us having peace, he mentioned our troubles in the *world* and then affirmed that he has overcome the world. That is where our peace comes from. He is our shepherd and our guardian and he is in charge!

In 1 John the author is talking about contrary spirits, those who would deny the divinity of Christ. In the middle of that conversation he confirmed that because we are from God we have overcome those spirits, *"because greater is he who is in you than he who is in the world."*[32] That has to be the text for Junior Asparagus' little reassuring song about God being bigger than the boogie man. Junior, by the way is one of the characters in the Veggie Tales series. I'd love to watch those writers at work some day. They must have a great time.

---

31   John 16:33
32   1 John 4:4

41

WE ARE OVERCOMERS!

One chapter after the "Greater is he" quote, John reit-erates: *"For whatever is born of God overcomes the world; and this is the victory that has overcome the world--our faith. Who is the one who overcomes the world, but he who believes that Jesus is the Son of God?"*[33]

We are believers and we have nothing to be afraid of. But sometimes we act in ways that deny the truth of that fact. Particularly to outsiders, we tend to look very afraid. We are afraid someone is taking our country in the wrong direction. We are afraid of the collapse of the American dream. We are afraid of Al- Qaeda and other terrorists. We are afraid that immigrants will ruin the good deal we've got – a bet-ter deal than most anyone else in the world. What we fail to understand is that God is bigger than all of that and more, And he is on our side. He has our back.

WHY ARE WE AFRAID?

Why are we afraid? Because we don't trust. And because of how we view this world in which we live. Have we never really sung and believed the old song

---

33   1 John 5:4-5

"This world is not my home"? We have put down roots here; unlike Abraham who just packed up and moved when God said "Go" without even knowing where he was headed.[34]

I love this nation. It is the best deal we could find or build on this earth. Could it be better? For sure. Could it be worse? Are you kidding? Have you read a newspaper or watched the news in the last ten years? In fact that's what we are afraid of, isn't it? That we will become what we read about in the rest of the world. Yet we need to understand that America is a part of the material world. Sisters and brothers, America is not our home. We are "…Just a passing through. Our treasures are laid up somewhere beyond the blue."[35]

We have been commissioned to make America as loving a place as we possibly can, but we are not charged with preventing its financial or military collapse. If we finish our lives sneaking around on Sundays to meet with other Christians for worship in order to avoid arrest by the ruling Muslim powers, we should understand that God is still in charge. And we can continue being his loving people is spite of what else is going on around us. Just like the little bird, singing away in the middle of the cat 5 storm.

---

34   Hebrews 11:8
35   Words and Music by Albert E .Brumley© 1965 -

DO NOT BE AFRAID

For us not to be afraid must be one of the most persistent parts of God's message to us. He must have understood the difficulty of that request. Over 60 times in the Old Testament he said to mankind, "Do not be afraid." And again in the New Testament he kept saying it, "Do not be afraid." Whether it was through Moses speaking to the people as they were preparing to go in and take the promised land,[36] or through an angel appearing to Mary to tell her of her future[37] the message was the same: we are not to be a fearful people. Reassuring the Israelites, Moses, speaking for God said, "He will not fail you or forsake you." That is still his reassurance to us today and his reminder of why it is that we are afraid. We are afraid because we do not trust that God will truly take all of what is happening in our horrible lives right now and will work it together for our good.[38] But he will. He promised. And he keeps his promises.

When the disciples woke Jesus up on the boat to calm the stormy sea, he had to calm his students first. *"Why are you afraid?"* he asked. And he accused them of

---

36   Deuteronomy 31:6
37   Luke 1:30
38   Romans 8:28

being of little faith.[39] You see that is the answer. We are afraid because our faith is weak. Our trust is weak. And when we are afraid, whether it is because of big scheme political reasons, or over the potential loss of a loved one to sickness or divorce, or because of the potential for financial loss or loss of face among our friends or coworkers, we need to ask God to increase our faith. And we should ask our friends to pray the same prayer for us.

Courage has to be a major part of the peace Jesus wanted to leave us with. But it is not a courage that comes from being sure of ourselves and our own abilities. When Moses spoke to Israel just before they went in to conquer the promised land, he told them to be strong and courageous, not because they were a powerful army or because the enemy was weak, but because God was going with them. He told them not to be afraid or tremble at their enemy "He will not fail you or forsake you," Moses said. God says we don't have anything to be afraid of because he has our back.

---

39   Matthew 8:25-27

CHAPTER 6

TAKE A BREAK AND LET
THE SPIRIT GET BACK IN FRONT

"He leadeth me, He leadeth me,
By His own hand He leadeth me,
His faithful follower I would be,
For by His hand, He leadeth me."[40]

I am sure you have heard this old story. There is a small group of hikers eating their lunch beside a mountain trail. Soon a man comes huffing and puffing up the trail and they invite him to stop for a rest. He says he can't and asks if they saw a group of Boy Scouts go up the mountain awhile ago. "I have to catch up with them," he explains, "I am their leader."

The story is often used to introduce a discussion of the nature of leadership, but I think it illustrates our relationship with the Spirit as well. Like the energetic young scouts, we want to run out in front. We don't need a leader – until we get into trouble that is.

THE SPIRIT LEADS US QUIETLY

We do so want to direct our own steps, to plan our own course, to map our own way. It is the American way. It is the American story. We start with the cards we are dealt and we play our way to the top. And we get to define the top: the top of our profession, the manager's job at work, the nicest house or car or boat in the neighborhood, the biggest TV among our friends.

But God says it is not in us.[41] That is not a put down. He is not saying we are not capable of developing a

---

41   Jeremiah 10:23

business plan and carrying it out. He is just saying that our vision is too limited to direct our spiritual lives. We cannot see what he can see.

ON TO PEACE

But his spirit will lead us to peace if we get out of the way. Peace is one of his promised fruits.[42] We need to quit being concerned about who and what people think we are. Isn't that a major part of what concerns us? What will my coworkers and friends think of me?

WHO ARE WE REALLY?

We need to figure out first of all who we really are. Some of us don't really know. We are so concerned with our image, so focused on what others think of us that we have not spent any time figuring out who we really are. We need to do that. We should be able to put it in a few words and know that it makes sense. And we need to put it in the context of what role God is calling us to play in his kingdom. What does he want us to accomplish for his work in our workplace, in our family, in our neighborhood, in our church and

---

42   Galatians 5: 22-23

civic club, among our golf or fishing partners? Once we have defined those roles, we have figured out who we really are – and who we are not.

That may be the hardest and most important part – figuring out who we are not. We are not defined by the roles we have been assigned at work or in the family, church or neighborhood. We are not the manager of so-and-so or the deacon of whatever. We are not the "head of the house" or the secretary of the board of such-and-such. We are instead ambassadors of God,[43] each of us with a separate set of good deeds programmed for us from the beginning of our time here on earth.[44]

"BE STILL AND KNOW"

How do we do that? How can we know what role God wants for us? Remember the story of Elijah? God wanted to speak to him. But God was not in the strong wind that passed by. Then an earthquake came, but God was not in the earthquake either. Then there was a fire, but God was not there either. As Elijah waited for God he was able to find him only in a still small voice.[45]

---

43   2 Corinthians 5:19-20
44   Ephesians 2:19
45   1 Kings 19:11-13

51

You see that is what we must do to find what God wants us to do. We must be still and listen.[46] We will have to know the scriptures because if we conclude that something is God's will for us but it is contrary to the written word of God, we can know that it is a thought that was planted by Satan. [47]

This will likely be some agonizing work and might take quite some time. Be patient. One of the fruits of the Spirit is patience.[48]

And pray. These are answers you cannot work out on your own. God's spirit has to show you the way. And work really hard at getting yourself out of the way. This is not about you. It is about your neighbors in the broadest, Biblical sense of that term.[49]

RESIGN FROM THE CAST OF THE PLAY

Once we have figured out who God wants us to be, and we have it firmly in our mind, and we are diligently working toward really being who we want to be and should be, we need to admit it to ourselves and others.

---

46   Psalms 46:10
47   1 John 4:1-3
48   Galatians 5:22-23
49   Luke 10:25-37

Quit trying to appear to be who you are not. That will be a hard thing for some of us. We have worked so hard, so long on our image that it has become a part of who we are. Breaking the habits connected with being someone else may be as hard as breaking a smoking or drinking habit. But with God's help, we can do it.

I need to pause here to ask you to think about your church family as well as your personal family, co-workers, neighbors, and friends. What is the image you have been trying to convey to your church? Who is it that you have wanted them to think you are? That may be an even harder role to break out of than the image you have been trying to convey at work.

We are all just people, but God loves us anyway. We all slip up. None of us has a right to claim salvation by our own doing. We are no better than those we seek to teach about the good news. Once we can own that fact, God can put us to work, and not until then.

MOVE YOUR FEET

But at that point, we need to be ready to move our feet. God can't use us very effectively if we are just sitting in a pew or if we are sitting on our couch at home with the doors locked. We need to plan how we are going to meet people in our neighborhoods and at our workplace. Someone has suggested that we should be doing things like being a repeat customer at the same establishments so we can get to know the clerks, joining a civic group or a hobby club, taking a class. That is, we need to be strategic about how we get to know people and about how best to represent God's love to those around us. Our prayer each morning should include something about how God will use us that day to show his love to others and to help someone who needs help.

CHAPTER 7

SET THE TONE; LIVE IN THE MOMENT

"So do not worry about tomorrow; for tomorrow will care for itself. Each day has enough trouble of its own." [50]

---

50   Matthew 6:34

I was recently at the funeral of an 18 year old girl. She was severely handicapped from birth and had not been expected to see her first birthday. The Rabbi conducting the service, her dad, and others who spoke mentioned the fact that Louise lived "in the moment" and they encouraged us to do the same. Louise had no choice. She never worried about what happened or didn't happen yesterday, nor was she concerned about what might happen tomorrow. She communicated with her caretakers and others through her huge smiles and her grunts and disagreeable looks.

The message to us was that we would gain by setting aside our concerns about the past and the future. Our friend Roberta has lived that way for the 17 years she has been working in Haiti. The motto she has lived by has been "God will provide." [51] She tells the story about sitting down to dinner with the children she had taken into her home to provide for them. There was no food in the house and one of the children asked. "What will we eat?" Her response was consistent with her life style, "God will provide." Soon there was a knock on the door and a neighbor was there with a live chicken – dinner!

---

51   Genesis 22:8

I am sure there have been similar times in your life when you got to the end of your rope, tied a knot to hold on, waited for God, and nothing happened. Those are the hardest. But he did promise. And he does sometimes take an opportunity to teach us patience and perseverance - though we wish he wouldn't bother. During the Sermon on the Mount Jesus taught that we shouldn't worry about what to eat, drink, or wear, but that we should seek his kingdom.[52] These are not metaphors about our next promotion. He is writing to Haitians who have good reason to be concerned about what to feed their children tonight. He is telling them not to worry about it; he will take care of it. And they look around and see their neighbors with nothing to put on the table. And he says to be concerned for their souls and for our own. Either we believe in a God who is in charge and who is able to keep promises and who will keep them, or we don't.

"And which of you by worrying can add a *single* hour to his life's span? If then you cannot do even a very little thing, why do you worry about other matters?"[53] The answer is, "Because we can." And maybe, "Because we must."

---

52   Matthew 6:31-34
53   Luke 12:25-26

Imagine "being concerned" about the health of a family member, on a situation at work, or a relationship issue and someone says, "Just relax; it will all work out for the best." Is that a relaxing direction, or doesn't it just add to our consternation? "Oh bother, now not only do I have to deal with all these issues in my life, but in addition I have to do it in a peaceful way!" I don't recommend going around telling people to relax. It probably won't help. But that is what God wants of us.

God wants us to love him and trust him and to know that he will take care of us in the long run. And knowing that and trusting him to keep his promises is what it takes to become a confident, peaceful representative of the truth and of the good news here on this earth.

CHAPTER 8

WHAT ARE CHRISTIANS REALLY CONCERNED ABOUT?

"Come to me, all who are weary and heavy-laden, and I will give you rest. Take my yoke upon you and learn from me, for I am gentle and humble in heart, and you will find rest for your souls. For my yoke is easy and my burden is light."[54]

---

54   Matthew 11:28-30

Awhile back I asked a group of Christian friends what they are worried about. One of them (a researcher, perhaps) was worried that my sample was small and was not random. But it is what it is and I would like to mention some of the responses here.

ARE WE BUSY ENOUGH?

A major group of responses was about whether we are doing enough. And that is a hard one for me as well. Even if we can quote the scriptures about it, like Ephesians 2:8-10, we still have a hard time putting them into action. Paul told the Ephesians in four different ways in verse 8 that we are not responsible for our salvation. 1) It is a gift; 2) it is not something we do ourselves; 3) it is not the result of anything we do; 4) we have no room to boast about it. But then he said we were created for good works. So he took the burden off with one hand and put it back on with the other. What are we supposed to do with that?

Here's what I've figured out about it. God wants us to fully understand that there is nothing we can do to earn our salvation. No matter how good we are, we are never good enough. Therefore there is no room for pride, and when we present the good news of salvation to those around us, we are telling them of a gift we have received, not of something we have accomplished.

Jesus wants all of us. He wants our heart, soul, mind, and strength.[55] Can we ever give Him enough? No. Does it make sense that we are concerned about not giving him enough? Yes. Can we take an afternoon off to play golf, go fishing, or read a book without feeling guilty for not knocking on doors, preaching on the street corner, or helping at the food pantry? I'm going to say a qualified, "Yes, we can take some time to ourselves." Let's look at the life of our example and teacher.

We don't know much about the first 30 years of Jesus' life. We do know that after the brief view we are given of the 12 year old boy Jesus, he grew in favor with men.[56] That indicates at least that he was not a boring preacher who was always serious about everything.

During the first miracle that John recorded, Jesus was at a wedding feast[57] and he attended several other feasts.[58] He invited himself to Zacchaeus' house for

---

55   **Luke 10:27**
56   Luke 2:52
57   John 2:1-11
58   e.g. Luke 14:1

dinner,[59] he was chastised for eating and drinking with sinners,[60] and he often used feasts in his illustrations.[61] But at the parties that found their way into the record, he did something significant with regard to his ministry. For example we would assume that he went to Zacchaeus' house to continue the discussion about the Spirit and baptism.

If we truly adopt Bill Hybels' "Just Walk Across the Room" strategy[62], we can go anywhere there are other people and assume that the Spirit will use us to help him move someone a little closer to the Lord that day.

So what about sitting under a tree or on a beach just thinking, or even choosing not to think? Or reading a novel? I really want to justify this one, because I love to be alone some of the time. I guess I'm technically an introvert because I get my energy more from being alone than from being with others. But as I searched the scripture I did not have to go far to discover this passage: "It is not good for the man to be alone. I will make a helper suitable for him."[63] And this one: "Also,

---

59   Luke 19:1-5
60   Luke 5:30
61   e.g. Luke 14:7-21
62   Bill Hybels: "Just Walk Across the Room, Zondervan, 2006
63   Genesis 2:18

if two lie down together, they will keep warm. But how can one keep warm alone?"[64]

Most Bible references to people being alone are of negative situations and being alone is a part of the negative situation. Jesus was alone a lot, but he was usually praying. And he said: *"A time is coming and in fact has come when you will be scattered, each to your own home. You will leave me all alone.* [A negative connotation to being alone.] *Yet I am not alone, for my Father is with me."*

The Bible seems to say that we should not strive to be alone. At least not for the long term or consistently. God intends for us, with the help of the Spirit, to be a support and a help for others.

On the other hand, if we are alone, God wants us to know that we are not alone. God is with us: "For none of us lives for ourselves alone, and none of us dies for ourselves alone. If we live, we live for the Lord; and if we die, we die for the Lord. So, whether we live or die, we belong to the Lord."

It is okay to "recharge" from time to time by being alone, but to seek to be alone through most of our lives

---

64   Ecclesiastes 4:11

is a waste of what God has given us. He intends for us to share with others.

What about Facebook and Twitter and other such means of interacting with people? If you are truly being interactive and not just spouting out your own thoughts, I would guess that God is okay with that, as long as it is in the context of a holy life.

SIMILAR WORRIES

Reproduced here are other responses from Christians about what bothers them. Many of them are serious concerns related to how we represent the church and God to the world around us. My answer to most of them is "God bless you for thinking about these things, and may his Spirit guide you as you work to improve in the areas you have identified. Please pray that I may be as serious as you have been in thinking about these things."

My message to you about these concerns is a hope that they will trigger in you a similar look inside your soul, an examination of your motivations, and a resolve to become more like Jesus day by day.[65]

---

65   2 Corinthians 4:16:

1. "I worry most often that I am not representing Christ as a positive ambassador that will draw people to him. I am disturbed by my tendency toward legalism instead of love."

2. "All the things the Lord tells us not to worry about. Mostly mammon. The economy, the environment, our health and health care, inflation and interest rates. For boomers - retirement; mostly stuff related to our own interests and wants. I would include the decline of morals and religious sentiment. Stagnation in our churches. Politics and the future of our nation."

3. "I have been thinking about your question. I assume (perhaps wrongly) you want the questions we are asking about our lives. In which case mine would be, "Am I where I am supposed to be or should I have already moved on? Should I be taking more initiative in determining what comes next in my life? Or should I sit back expecting that God will do with me what he wills?"

4. "Church-wise there is something that disturbs me much. While your question is a good one, I read in several of our magazines the question and answer sections and note that the questions we seem consumed with and I am concerned that they reveal a non-flattering perception of the Lord. I remember

the question, Should a teenager with purple hair be allowed to wait on the Lord's Table? The questions that are put forward assume a God that is legalistic, expecting us to jump through a plethora of hoops to receive his blessings, rather than the God described in the Bible who is love and desires that all men be saved."

5. "Do I take myself too seriously? It seems that the more serious we take our selves the less we can understand grace and the absurdity of the world."

6. "In our materialistic, self-centered society do I look any different? Am I just "playing" safe church without ever getting drastically, radically, passionately serious about saving souls and doing the hard stuff to make that happen. What disturbs me is trying to fit God into my world instead of me fitting into His."

7. "I guess I worry about developing poor health--I think none of us want to be a burden to others [this is probably an age thing]. I think, mainly, I worry about not recognizing opportunities to be of service to others or share with them about our God."

8. "You asked, 'What are Christians uptight about? What worries us? Disturbs us?' There are so many places to start, but I will start with this: Most Christians

are uptight with the way the world system has taken over the control of the universe. But this does not have to be, because God promised if we would humble ourselves, turn from our sinful ways, He will hear from heaven and will heal our land. Most Christians do not want to take the time to build a relationship with God to the point that no matter what is going on in his or her life, they know that they are not alone and help is only a prayer a way. Christians are worried about the economic situation and what will happen to their future. Again, God promised that he would take care of his children no matter what is going on around us. Most Christians try to deal with God on a human level and forget that God is spirit and you must worship him in spirit and truth. As Christians, we are disturbed because we don't get answers to our problems and circumstances right away, so we begin to doubt God and his word. No matter what happens now or in the future, we must stay true to God and our position as a Christian, we are God's examples to who he really is. If we fold and give up, some people in the world will never get to know who God is. Hope I did not go too far off the track of what you were asking for. :-)" [Not at all - DMM]

9. "The worries that we communicate to the world at large are about abortion, gay marriage, evolution, and negative influences on young people (sex, drugs,

etc.). In settings where Christians are sharing their behind-the-scenes worries with each other, I also hear about church growth and - occasionally - Muslims taking over the world. I'm hoping though that Christians who worry are also concerned about more personal things like sin in their own lives and whether their friends and family are walking with God, but unfortunately, those aren't the ones that are usually expressed."

10. "I was thinking about this as I fell asleep last night. I'm not sure if you are doing this by age group, but I would think that matters. So for the record, I will be 53 in a few weeks. Here are a few big things that try to bog me down on a daily basis:

a. We worry about health issues both for ourselves and parents. Healthcare for aging and dying parents are huge issues for me and my peers.
b. Grief and loss. Doing it and doing it well.
c. As Christians, we are confronted with ugly battles. I think particularly for those of us in any kind of ministry, Satan is working overtime to discourage, threaten, and defeat us.
d. I also believe that Satan works overtime on trying to isolate us....he will do anything to destroy relationships especially in the church.

e. If you are a member of the church of Christ, then you are constantly aware of the differing opinions about worship. This wears me out. "

11. "That the world will end soon and we need to have the sense of urgency to share and live the Gospel message. Another, that Seeking and saving the lost must be the work of the church; its primary work, as it was for Jesus. Another, to restore the New Testament church."

12. "I've tried very hard to give up worrying. It's a waste of time and usually the things people worry about don't happen ... something else happens that they didn't even think to worry about. I don't know that worry is the right word for me. It's more of a "concern" that I do my best to turn over to God since I have no control of the matter ... but it would be the faithfulness of my children and grandchildren that will ultimately lead them to salvation and keep them in a saved state. I preface the next statement with the understanding that God is in control and whatever happens in our country, God will ultimately cause good to result. But the state of our country and the world is worrisome. If I catch myself worrying (or being concerned) about something, I'll let you know."

13. "After reading the list....now I am really worried. I should have mentioned that I worry that I won't have the energy that I want and need on mission trips!!!"

14 "Some of my concerns are: "Am I doing enough?"; "Will my children be faithful?"; "Am I planting enough 'seeds' that will germinate & grow?". It is truly difficult to "be anxious for nothing".

CHAPTER 9

WARNING ABOUT PART 2

"They took his advice; and after calling the apostles in, they flogged them and ordered them not to speak in the name of Jesus, and then released them. So they went on their way from the presence of the Council, rejoicing that they had been considered worthy to suffer shame for His name. And every day, in the temple and from house to house, they kept right on teaching and preaching Jesus as the Christ."[66]

---

66   Acts 5:40-42

I need to clarify what comes next lest someone think I am wimping out on speaking the truth to those who need to hear it. We are called on to be bold proclaimers of the truth. When Jesus' body left the earth, He put his followers in charge of spreading the good news.[67] A short time later they were hauled in before the religious leaders of the day, were beaten and then commanded not to speak in his name. They immediately went back to the most public place in the city and resumed preaching and teaching.

Jesus wants us to be bold speakers too. He wants us confidently telling the truth about who he is and what God requires of us. But he wants us to be peaceable and gentle about it. And nowhere has he charged us with forcing people into submission to his will.

In the next two chapters I write about fourteen specific issues of the day. For each of them I apply the principle that God wants us leading people to repentance rather than forcing them into submission through legislation. You may agree or disagree, but please do not conclude that I lack courage. Consider instead what God said about it:

---

67   Acts 1:6-8

"For the word of the cross is foolishness to those who are perishing, but to us who are being saved it is the power of God. For it is written, ' I WILL DESTROY THE WISDOM OF THE WISE, AND THE CLEVERNESS OF THE CLEVER I WILL SET ASIDE.'"

"Where is the wise man? Where is the scribe? Where is the debater of this age? Has not God made foolish the wisdom of the world? For since in the wisdom of God the world through its wisdom did not come to know God, God was well-pleased through the foolishness of the message preached to save those who believe. For indeed Jews ask for signs and Greeks search for wisdom; but we preach Christ crucified, to Jews a stumbling block and to Gentiles foolishness, but to those who are the called, both Jews and Greeks, Christ the power of God and the wisdom of God. Because the foolishness of God is wiser than men, and the weakness of God is stronger than men". [68]

Whole books, longer than this one could be written about each of the following topics. This list is intended as thought provokers or discussion starters and as an illustration of the principle that God has called us to change the world through preaching and teaching, not through legislating.

---

68   1 Corinthians 1:18-25

One more thing before we dive in. In the next few pages I speak of being friendly to all people who may want to worship with us. There I am saying that we should invite all comers into our worship services, but not to stay the same. Rather to grow with us in righteousness and in their love for God and mankind.

PART 2

PEACE AND POLITICS

God has not called us to use the country's police forces to require non-believers to live righteously. Instead, he has charged us with calling people to righteousness.

CHAPTER 10

STICKING MY NECK OUT

*"Be anxious for nothing, but in everything by prayer
and supplication with thanksgiving let your requests
be made known to God. And the peace of God, which
surpasses all comprehension, will guard your hearts and
your minds in Christ Jesus.*[69]*"*

In the next two chapters, I plan to be more specific about some of the things that worry us most, and in doing so to apply the principles we have discussed so far. But first let me recap the principles:

1. God loves us and wants us to be at peace.[70]

2. Though he wants us to be busy in his kingdom,[71] he does not require that we "fix" the world. That's his job.[72]

3. God has not called us to use the country's police forces to require non-believers to live righteously. Instead, he has charged us with calling people to righteousness.

God wants us working toward righteousness, which includes justice for the poor and disadvantaged.[73] But he doesn't want us so obsessed by our outcomes (or lack thereof) that it destroys our peace. So what are we to do about the issues of the day?

---

70   John 14:27
71   Ephesians 2:10
72   2 Peter 3:10-13: Revelation 21:1
73   Isaiah 58:6-7

What should our attitude be toward the following?

1. MUSLIM PEOPLE?

We are to love them; they are our neighbors. They are represented in the scripture by the outsider, the Samaritan, who stopped to help when the religious leaders failed to do so.[74] If Jesus went into Samaria and asked a woman for help[75], surely we can go into a Muslim neighborhood and offer to give some assistance.

2. TERRORISTS?

We are not likely to meet any and to know who they are, but if Jesus could pray for his murderers ("Father forgive them...") we can pray for terrorists. And I am not suggesting we pray for their destruction. That is not what Jesus did. He prayed for their salvation.

3. SOCIAL LEGISLATION AND THE GOVERNMENT?

What do we know about the Bible's writings on the role of Christians and government? One thing we do

---

74   Luke 10:30-37
75   John 4:7

know is that democracy or a republican form of government was unknown in that day, so what is written there is more likely relevant to a dictatorial system. Jesus said we should pay our taxes, so, even though a couple of his followers were zealots who previously had sought to overthrow Rome, that was not his approach. Paul reiterated Jesus' instruction and expanded on it,[76] saying that we should be subject to the government and that to resist it was the same as opposing God. So joining illegal resistance movements, as exciting and adventurous as that sounds, is not an option for a Christian. Speaking the truth though, even from billboards, TV ads, blogs, and Facebook pages, is a Christian option - one we should strongly consider as a viable part of our Christian witness to the world.

But what do we do in a democratic nation? How do we exercise our democratic rights? Can we run for office? Should we push for "Christian" legislation? Here are my answers; you should study it out for yourself:

4. PUBLIC OFFICE?

The Spirit prepares us all and calls us to many different roles in our society. If you feel drawn to public service, even in an elected office, you should consider it. Just

---

76   Romans 13:1-7

be aware of the tools Satan will use against you, if you are elected.

A. **Power**.

Lord Acton is often quoted as saying, "Power corrupts." Most Biblical references to power refer to the power of God. Power is addictive and that explains why people continue to run for high office long after anyone thinks they have any chance of winning. People who have power tend to think they should use it and they often do so to their own detriment and that of others.

b. Pride.

"Pride goes before destruction."[77] Pride shows up in lots of ways. It lowers resistance to sexual temptation and to temptation to appropriate what is not ours for our own purposes. It takes an "I am worth it!" approach to life and promotes a sense of "I am smart enough to get away with this; besides, look at all I have given up for my constituents."

c. The Value of Christian Leaders.

In spite of the many possible pitfalls, a Christian leader who truly acts like one would be a welcome relief and

---

77   Proverbs 16:18-19

a tremendous asset to the kingdom. She or he would act and vote on principle regardless of which way the political winds are blowing and would daily risk not being reelected in favor of doing the right thing.

5. "RIGHTEOUS LEGISLATION?"

This may be a little controversial, but I do not believe that, as Christians, we are called on to pass laws or to try to get others to pass laws legislating our morality onto the rest of society. God wants us all to be free moral agents, to make our own decisions about whether or not to follow him. Otherwise he could have put an electric fence around the tree in the middle of the garden, with razor wire on top, and placed some scary looking guards by it.

We are charged with bringing people to Jesus, not with forcing them through legislation and law enforcement to do God's will. Didn't we learn that lesson after the prohibition of alcohol in the 1920's? And the time known as the "dark ages" was a time when the church got control of the government and everyone was, at least in name, a Christian. We do not want to go back to that time. Every soul that is saved is one less person we have to worry about trying to force to follow

PEACE ON EARTH?

God's will. We make followers by preaching,[78] not by legislating!

6. DEGRADATION OF THE CHURCH?

The church seems to be falling apart. It is divided; it is off-focus; it has been captured by charlatans and is being misrepresented; it is rapidly falling away from the truths of the scripture. What are we to do? Do you hear echoes of Chicken Little? "The sky is falling! The sky is falling!"

Yes the church has its issues, just as did most of the churches addressed by the letters of the New Testament and five of the seven churches addressed in the Revelation. No we can't relax our efforts just because church problems have been around for over 2000 years. But neither do we need to cry out in defeat.

We are called on to the stay the course. "Preach the gospel,[79]" Paul told Timothy. "In season; out of season." Keep preaching. Don't give up. I remember Kinwood Devore, the minister at the Metropolitan Church of Christ and the Executive Director of Metropolitan Fresh Start in San Francisco, teaching a group of urban

78   1 Corinthians 1:21
79   2 Timothy 4:1-2

90

ministry fanatics a song, and with it an idea. The title was "Never give up!" Brother Kinwood said his group started every gathering with that song.

We are not called to rail against sociological phenomena, we are called on to teach the truth. And by teaching the truth, we will convert people to Jesus, even perhaps those who have worn his name in vain. But failing that, we will hold up a standard that the world will relate to. We will represent our savior in and to this world in which we live. Drop the rant, pick up the Bible and let's preach - gently, calmly, with the confidence that comes with our salvation.

7. THE ECONOMY?

We know better than this. Right out of the gate, Jesus in the sermon on the mount told us that God takes care of the birds and flowers and he will take care of us.[80] He told us he had never seen God's children begging bread.[81]

But we have become dependent on the U.S. economy. We get angry when economic forces take our jobs overseas. We rant when some rich people get richer by

80   Matthew 6:26
81   Psalm 37:25

cheating less fortunate people - especially if it is us they are cheating. We are afraid that immigrants will take jobs away from us, that the economy is going into the toilet and that all our "things" will follow it there.

We just need to trust that God will keep his promise. We should be living on what he puts in our hands, giving away as much as we can, working to support ourselves and our families, and telling people the good news. Everything else is icing. That includes Medicare and Social Security, a solvent government, our retirement savings and anything else we may be counting on. Set it all aside and trust.

CHAPTER 11

CLOSER TO HOME

God loves us and wants us to be at peace.
-And-
*Though he wants us to be busy in his kingdom, he does
not require that we "fix" the world. That's his job.*
-And-
*God has not called us to use the country's police forces to
require non-believers to live righteously. Instead, he has
charged us with calling people to righteousness*

This next set of issues may be closer to your heart than those in Chapter 10. Perhaps you have had to deal with one or more of these first hand. You may view my answers as just that - my answers, but I believe they are based on the three principles listed above. Some of the scriptural references for the principles are in the first part of Chapter 10.

1. ABORTION

When is a baby not a baby? That is the question isn't it? Almost everyone agrees that we shouldn't be killing babies, so the argument has turned into one about the "personhood" of the unborn.

But the argument is not real. If a baby is a baby when it is born, why is it not a baby 7 minutes before it is born, or 7 hours, or 7 days, or 7 months? At whatever stage of development, what is in a mother's womb is at some point in becoming a person. Once you decide that you want to justify putting it to death you put yourself in the position of having to determine when is the baby really a baby and when is it not. There is no scientific way to make that determination. Whatever day you pick in the process of development, some-one can legitimately ask, "Why not a day earlier - or later?"

Having said that, the proper approach for a Christian, and therefore for the church, is to teach, not to legislate. Minnesota Citizens Concerned for Life has an excellent billboard campaign in this regard.[82] They do not accuse people of murder, or in any other way put people down. Instead, they hold up the importance of respecting life - even when it is still in the womb.

Our assigned role is to teach, not to legislate.

2. GAY MARRIAGE

Who is and is not welcome in your church service? A lot of us have signs and letterheads that proclaim, "Everyone Welcome." Does that include a gay couple? If sinners are not welcome, would we turn away a lying politician or a cheating business person?

How many gay or lesbian people do you know? How many are you likely to meet in the circles you move in? Is being in a gay relationship really worse than living with your girlfriend or boyfriend? How would you go about sharing the gospel gently with someone

---

82   http://www.mccl.org/page.aspx?pid=646

who is in a gay relationship or who suspects he might
be gay?

These are complex questions. Here are some of my
thoughts. We are all sinners.[83] Some of us recognize
that fact and some do not. Some of us are belligerent
about our sin. We want to defend our right to stay in
it. We need to be taught, but are unwilling to listen.
That makes it very difficult to reach some people, and
as Jesus' "seed planters"[84] we often decide what kind
of soil is in front of us and we decide not to plant any
seed.

We do not seem to be nearly as upset with people in
our community who are living with a partner of the
opposite sex as we are with those who are living with
someone of the same sex. If we are to be a church that
is actively "seeking and saving the lost" we do need to
be welcoming to sinners. That is not an easy transition
for many of us.

What should be our stand on gay marriage legislation?
Again, it is not our assignment to legislate people into
righteousness. Marriage is a religious institution that
has traditionally been reinforced by the state. If every
state and every nation endorses gay marriage it will not

83   Romans 3:23
84   Mark 4:13-14

change God's mind about it. Marriage in God's eyes is one man and one woman. We spread that idea by gentle teaching, not by passing laws.

Our responsibility is to love people and to teach them gently.

3. IMMIGRATION

God said:

a. *"You shall not oppress a stranger, since you yourselves know the feelings of a stranger, for you also were strangers in the land of Egypt;"*[85] and

b. *"The LORD protects the strangers; He supports the father-less and the widow;"*[86] and

c. *"A widow is to be put on the list only if she is not less than sixty years old, having been the wife of one man, having a reputation for good works; and if she has brought up children, if she has shown hospitality to strangers, if she has washed the saints' feet, if she has assisted those in distress, and if she has devoted herself to every good work;"*[87] and

---

85   Exodus 23:9
86   Psalm 146:9
87   1 Timothy 5:9-10

d. "Now when you reap the harvest of your land, you shall not reap to the very corners of your field, nor shall you gather the gleanings of your harvest. [10] Nor shall you glean your vineyard, nor shall you gather the fallen fruit of your vineyard; you shall leave them for the needy and for the stranger. I am the LORD your God."[88]

So, how can we as His people join our voices with those who are saying, "Stay away."

I do know that immigration is scary. We are afraid. We are scared that uncontrolled immigration will adversely affect our standard of living. "They" will come here and get the jobs we and our children wanted. "They" will bring disease, crime, and immorality into "our" culture.

The truth of it all is that God is bigger than all that. We are to trust him and welcome the strangers

Some will say that they oppose immigrants because they are coming here in opposition to our laws. But we have passed laws that have set up constraints on who can come and who must stay away. And those constraints are along economic and racial lines. That invokes for me all the scripture that says we are to

---

88   Leviticus 19:9

become advocates for the poor, especially for those who are being taken advantage of by people in power.[89]

4. WAR

Christians preach that when someone hits us, we should offer them the other cheek to hit that one as well.[90] We teach forgiveness of our enemies.[91] When they came to capture Jesus in the garden Jesus had Peter put away his sword.[92]

Yet from our correspondence, one would think that we are war mongers. This is a difficult issue. We do not want to be identified with those citizens who treated our returning Viet Nam Vets with disrespect and dishonor.

A few days ago I was in a grocery store wearing my USMC hat. As frequently happens, a man stopped me to inquire about my service. Whether it was for three years or for thirty, Marines always are inquisitive about another Marine's service. Noticing my gray hair, he

---

89   e.g,: Psalm 82:2-4;, Proverbs 31:8-9; Isaiah 1:17; Isaiah 25:3-5;
          Isaiah 58:5-7
90   Matthew 5:39
91   Matthew 5:44
92   John 18;10-11

asked whether I had been in Viet Nam. It turned out we had both served there and we went through the routine, when, where, and with what unit. As we finished our brief conversation, without thinking about it, I said to him, "Welcome home." Without hesitation he repeated the familiar greeting. On the way out of the store Charlene identified what had happened. "No one else would welcome you home, so you welcome each other."

We do want to respect our young people who go off to war to protect our freedoms, and Paul did say that government bears the sword legitimately.[93] I do not have all the answers to this one. But this I do know. We are called on to be a peace loving people. As Christians our first and perhaps our only weapon is the metaphorical sword of God: his word, the Bible. We should not be leading the charge to go off killing people in another part of the world. We should instead be trying to teach the truth in "all the world."[94]

5. THE EDUCATION OF OUR CHILDREN

One of our principle concerns today is whether our children are receiving a proper education. Many are

---

93   Romans 13:1-7
94   Mark 16:15-16

concerned that we are falling behind other nations, particularly in math and science. But Christians' major complaint is the secularization of the schools - excluding any reference to God.

Here is the basic problem. We turned schooling over to the government years ago, and in doing so we relinquished control over the education of our children. The schools are no longer seen as extensions of the family to accomplish family goals. They are now viewed as extensions of the government to accomplish national goals. And as the society grew more secular, so did the national goals as played out through the school system.

Why are *they* not properly educating *our* children? The question more properly should be, "Why aren't we educating our children?" Yes, we live in a complex world and education is more involved than it was when language arts and a little basic math were all that was required, but we also have many more resources under our control than we did back then.

The early home schoolers have done a lot of the work gaining legitimacy for the approach in every state. Many states now have approved a free or inexpensive on-line curriculum for homeschoolers. Can't afford to give up an income to free up time to home school? I would encourage you to assess whether it is a matter of "can't" or is it instead a situation where you are wanting to maintain a lifestyle you have established for yourself?

If you are a single parent working to put food on the table there are still options. Churches, intead of railing against the government should be helping with this issue: creating affordable, perhaps even free resources for education. Cooperative arrangements can go a long way in this regard. Worried about the quality of the home school education? Do some research. Home schoolers are taking top honors in contests like spelling bees and are gaining admission to the top schools in the nation.

On the other hand, all of my kids and grandkids have been in the public school system. If we choose that option we need to acknowledge that it was our own choice. We need to adequately prepare our kids for what they will encounter there. And we need to encourage efforts like those of high schoolers who meet at the flag pole for a brief prayer before the day starts.

Let's quit complaining and do something productive about the issue.

6. SALVATION

Oddly, Christians continue to express concern about whether they will go to heaven. They have read the book. Intellectually they know the answers. Paul told the Ephesians that they cannot earn salvation; it is a gift. Yet still Christians worry. We worry about whether we are doing enough. Even if we aren't concerned about missing heaven, we still are worried that we are not making a sufficient effort for the kingdom.

It may be that we just don't trust God's promises, but I will suggest that the primary reason for all this concern is that we really are living our lives with one foot in the kingdom of God and the other foot in Satan's world. We have not dedicated our lives to Jesus. We are spending most of our time here earning a living, increasing our standard of living and trying to keep up with the debt we have created. Then we worry that we are not doing enough to further the kingdom of God. Brothers and Sisters, if this is the case, it is time we got serious about being God's army on this earth. He said we should deny ourselves and daily take up our figurative cross. It is no wonder we feel guilty if we have not made an effort to live up to his standards.

7. The Salvation of our Families and Others We Care About.

And we are worried about the salvation of our families. People we care deeply about do not share our love for God or for his principles. They may be loving, giving people but they do not give God the credit, nor do they depend on him for their sense of well being. Maybe we made some mistakes when they were younger or when we first met them. Or perhaps we are uncertain how much to say to them now. Is there more we could be doing?

God does require something of us in our relations with other people. He wants us to love them and to teach them. He wants us to tell them the good news. But there our responsibility stops. God has not asked us to make people obey him or to browbeat them into subission. Even if we could do so (and likely we cannot), it would not be real. It would not be in keeping with God's requirement for people to come to him and to follow him of their own free will.

We are free to grieve over those who have chosen not to follow Jesus. Jesus wept over the City of Jerusalem. But, if we are gently teaching and are setting a good example, if we have made the truth clear, we are not to be worried that there is something else we shoud be doing. The Holy Spirit of God has been charged with leading people to him[95] and we are not to take over his job.

We hear often that the church is losing its kids. That seems to be true, but I would point out another way to look at it. The church that is losing its kids is the institutional church - the one you can see, the one that is measured by attendance. I would question whether Jesus is losing so many of his followers. I would guess that he never had them in the first place. Yes they may have been faithful attenders, but I doubt that many of them ever truly gave their lives to Jesus. My observation is that those young people who have been called by their local church to go outside the church building, to get into the streets, either here or in foreign countries, to tell good news and to help people who need help, keep doing that in the name of the Lord after they grow up.

---

95   Titus 3:5

CHAPTER 12

SO WHAT?

"And the seed whose fruit is righteousness is sown in peace by those who make peace.[96]*"*

If we get this right, what effect will it have on the world around us?

BETTER CHRISTIANS

As we come to be at peace in the world, living in it, but not being of it, we will be able to act confidently on God's instructions.

Some of Jesus' teachings are downright terrifying. "Drop your business and come follow me." "Sell everything you have worked so hard to accumulate, give it to the poor and come follow me." If you are not convinced, get a copy of David Platt's book, "Radical."

Telling people the good news is scary for lots of reasons. Going intentionally to strange places, even in the city where we live, can be very intimidating. But as we condition ourselves to be confident in the promises God has made to us, we will become more bold in our outreach. That is not to say that we will become more aggressive as we move toward people. In spite of the soldier analogies, Jesus did not call on us to be belligerent.[97] But we will present ourselves more confidently. We will gain respect because of our integ-

---

97   Ephesians 4:1-3

rity. Even people who disagree with us will respect our honesty and reliability. We will become more worthy as conduits of God's message to his people. We will be better family members, employees, employers and church members.

BETTER CHURCHES

Imagine a church made up of confident non-worriers who are clear about God's will for them and are busy in the community around them telling the good news and helping people who need help. Or, if you have trouble with that image, imagine a church with several people like that who are also gently teaching the rest of the group to become like they are as they follow Jesus.

It will be a powerful group, not because of its own power but because it draws on the power of him who has overcome the world[98]. They will be active and loving and gentle and very busy in the work of the Lord.

A BETTER WORLD

With churches full of people who are gently telling good news and are helping others through their hard

---

98   John 16:33

times - moving with confidence through the world - how could the world not be a better place?

SUMMARY

Faith in God includes trust in his promises. He promised he would take care of us just as he does the lilies (and the dandelions). If we believe that promise, we can turn loose of our dependence on ourselves and on things we have accumulated. It will free us to live in the moment; to do what is right, right now.

And if we trust in the power of God, we can let go of our worries about the world around us. Let go of the worries and put our energies instead to doing what we can to make it a better place.

Keep in mind three principles:

1. God loves us and wants us to be at peace.

2. Though he wants us to be busy in his kingdom, he does not require that we "fix" the world. That's his job.

3. God has not called us to use the country's police forces to require non-believers to live righteously.

Instead, he has charged us with calling people to righteousness.

If we will busy ourselves with doing what God has called us to do, going to where people are, telling the good news to everyone we meet, and helping those who need help, he will give us the peace that is beyond comprehension, and that will cause others to ask where it comes from.

May God bless you as you put this to work.

ACKNOWLEDGEMENTS

Again to my dear wife, who continues to put up with me.

To my friends who read the draft. As a result of their comments, I have made some changes to try to soften it somewhat (really!), to clarify some points, and to make it clearer that I am not calling on people to keep quiet about the truth.

The reviewers were Ann Baur, Dan Horn, Jeff Lambert, Linda Lingo, and Charlene May. Their reviewer role does not imply that they agree with the content.

And to diane michele may who created the cover art and to her son, David, who served as the model.

91771462R00065

Made in the USA
Columbia, SC
23 March 2018